first trio album

for three violins

Compiled, Arranged, and Edited
by HARVEY S. WHISTLER and HERMAN A. HUMMEL

CONTENTS

		Page
TRIO BRILLANTE	Dancla	22
TRIO-CAPRICE	Dancla	5
TRIO DE BALLET	Hoffmann	19
TRIO DE CONCERT	Mazas	6
TRIO DE SALON	Hohmann	3
TRIO DE VALSE	Hermann	7
TRIO DIVERTIMENTO	Eichberg	24
TRIO DRAMATIQUE	Blumenthal	18
TRIO ELÉGANTE	Blumenthal	16
TRIO ÉLÉGIAQUE	Eichberg	10
TRIO-FINALE	Tours	32
TRIO-IMPROMPTU	Hoffmann	28
TRIO IN B♭	Eichberg	14
TRIO IN C	De Beriot	2
TRIO IN D	Grünwald	12
TRIO IN F	Wohlfahrt	8
TRIO IN G	Schradieck	4
TRIO LYRIQUE	De Beriot	29
TRIO-NOVELLETTE	Eichberg	17
TRIO PASTORALE	Mazas	15
TRIO PERPETUO	Tours	26
TRIO POPULAIRE	Eichberg	20
TRIO SCHERZANDO	Hermann	30
TRIO-SERENADE	Mazas	9
TRIO SYNCOPÉ	Tours	13

Rubank

HAL•LEONARD
CORPORATION

Trio in C

DE BERIOT

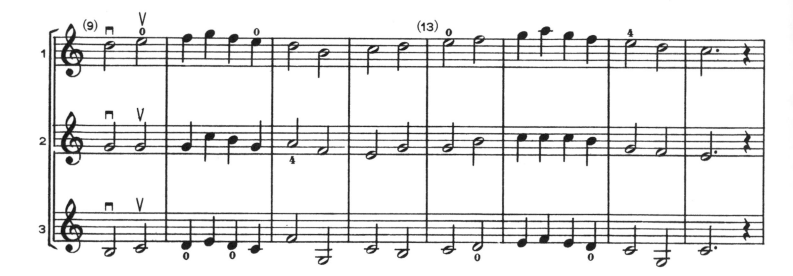

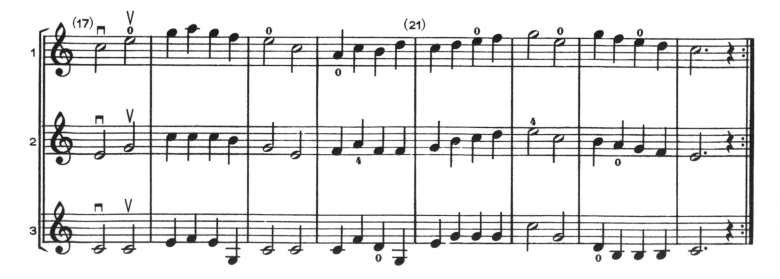

1363-31

Trio de Salon

HOHMANN

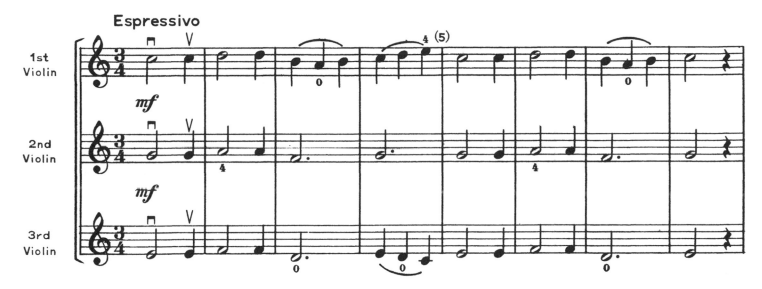

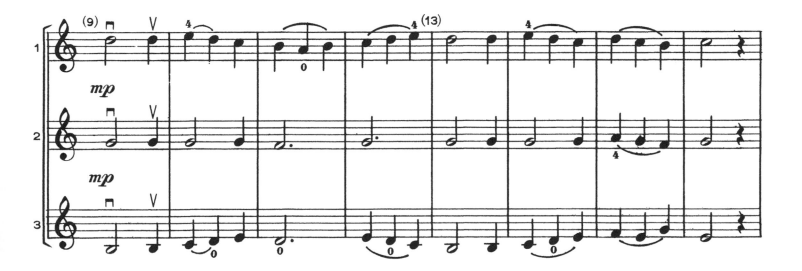

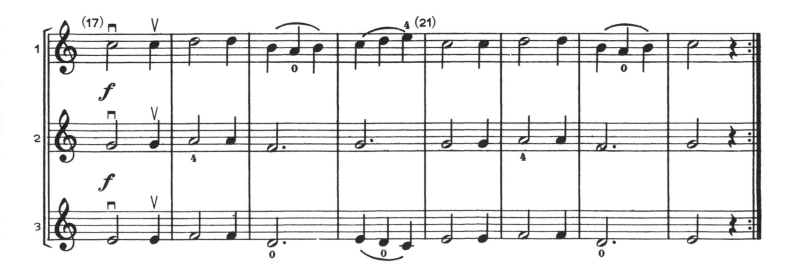

Trio in G

SCHRADIECK

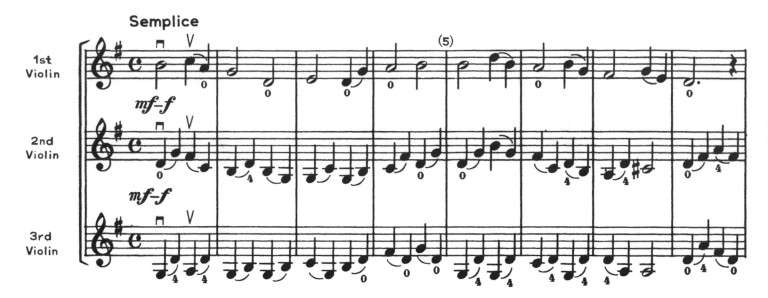

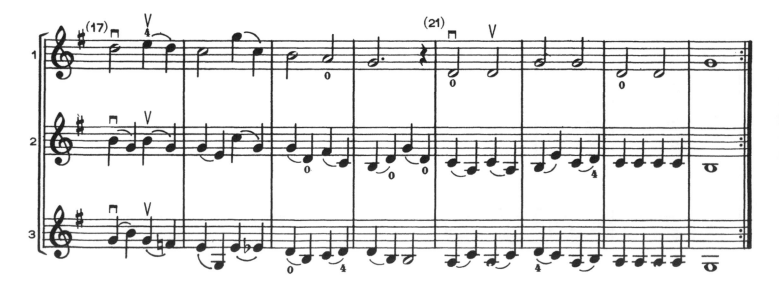

Trio - Caprice

DANCLA

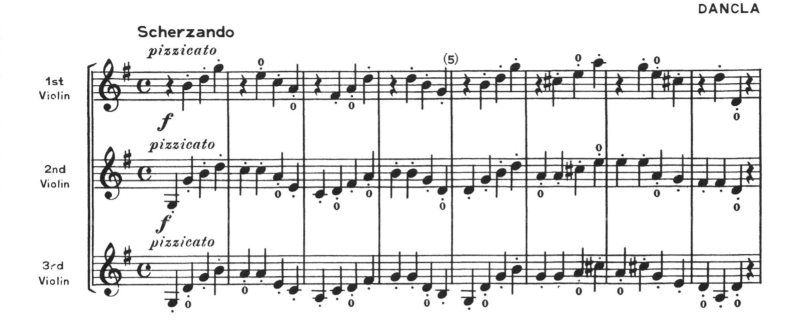

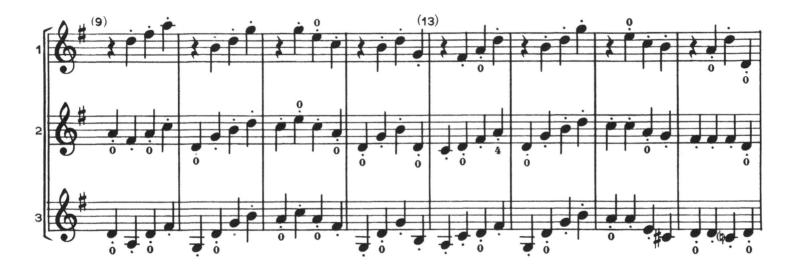

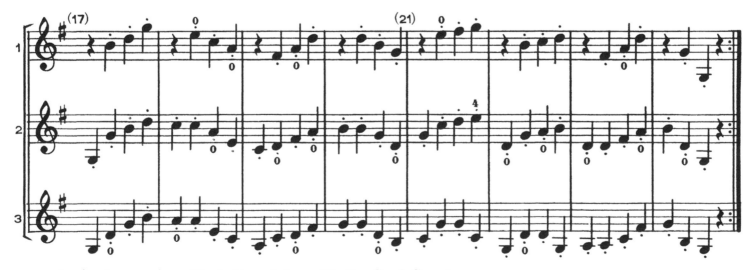

pizzicato, or *pizz.* = Pluck the string with the first finger.

Trio de Concert

MAZAS

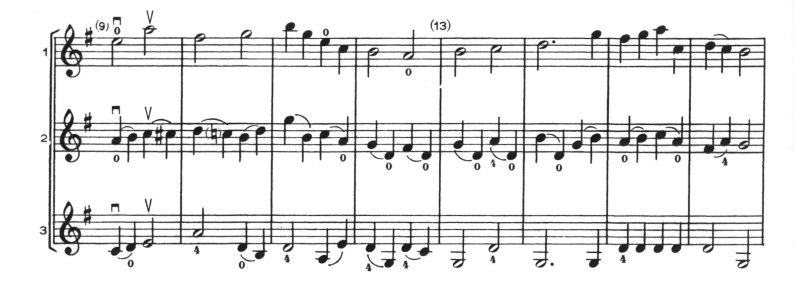

Trio de Valse

HERMANN

Andante cantabile

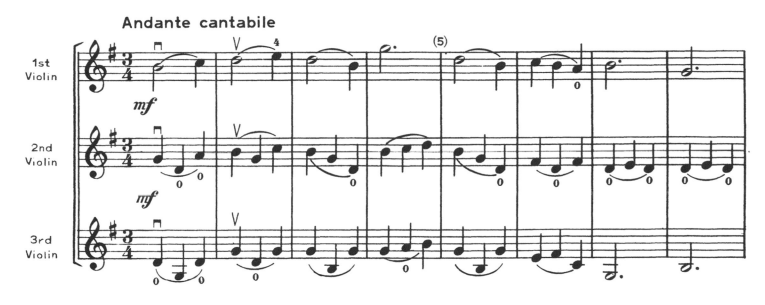

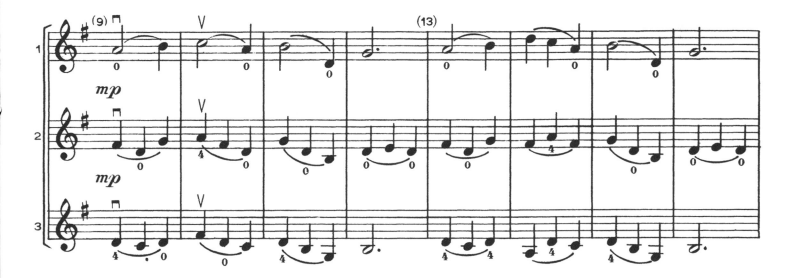

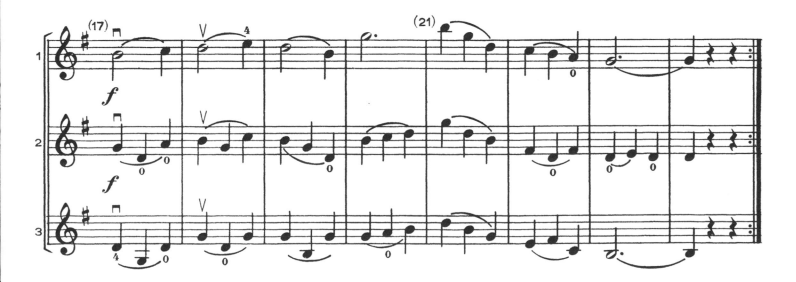

1363-31

Trio in F

WOHLFAHRT

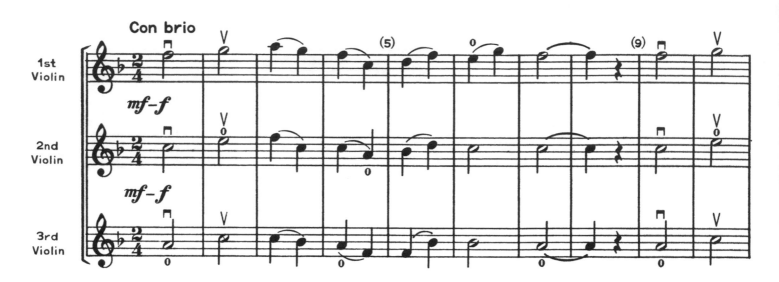

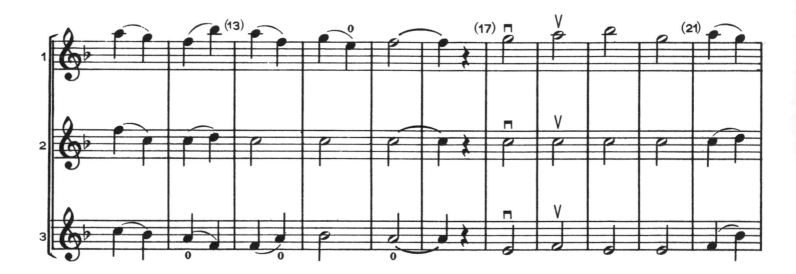

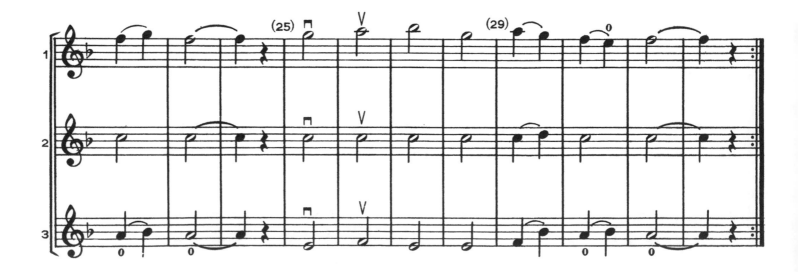

Trio - Serenade

MAZAS

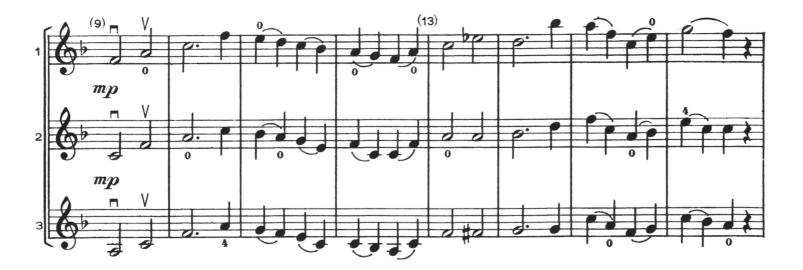

Trio Élégiaque

EICHBERG

Grazioso

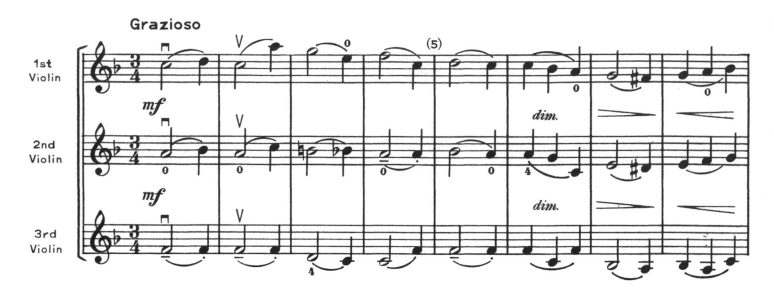

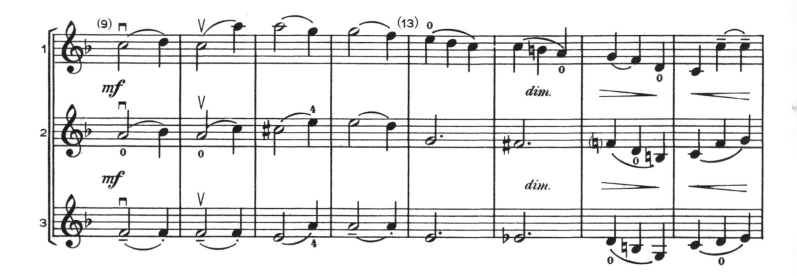

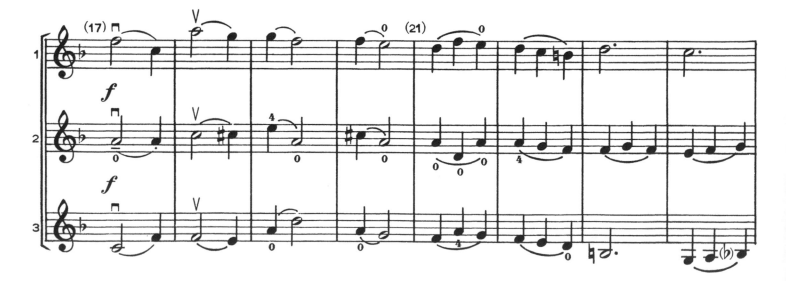

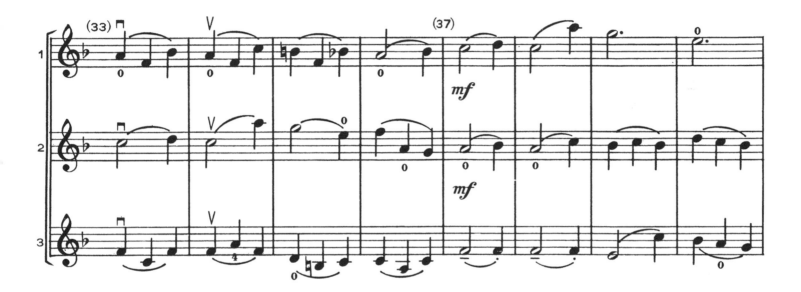

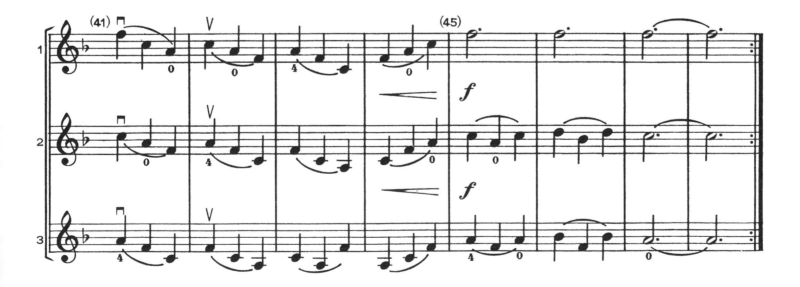

Trio in D

GRÜNWALD

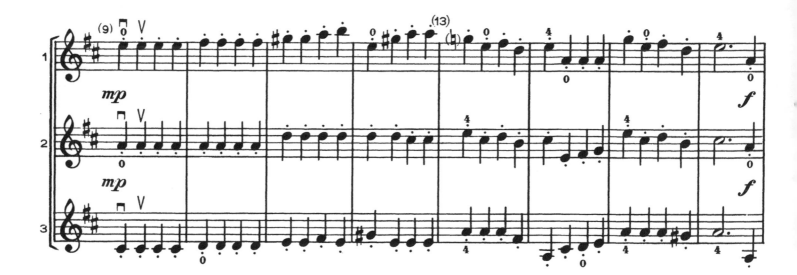

Trio Syncopé

TOURS

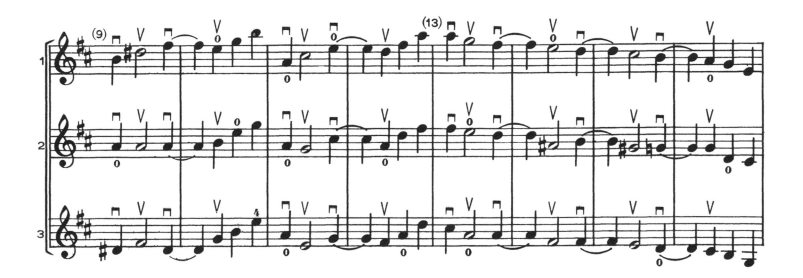

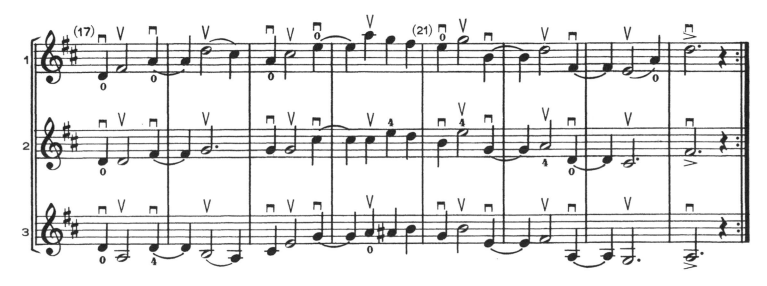

Trio in B♭

EICHBERG

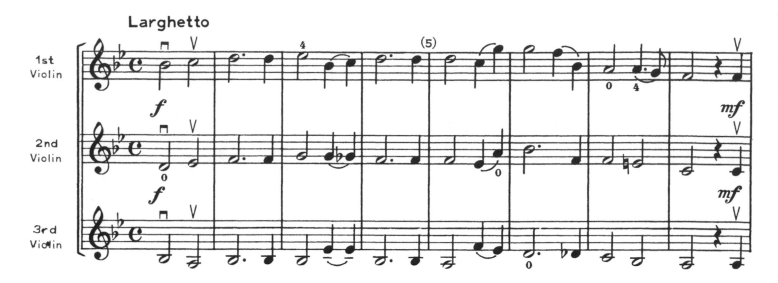

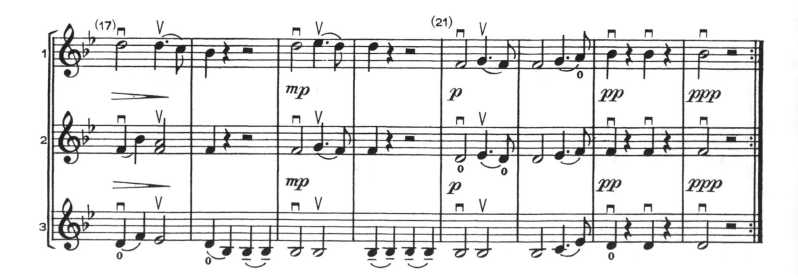

Trio Pastorale

MAZAS

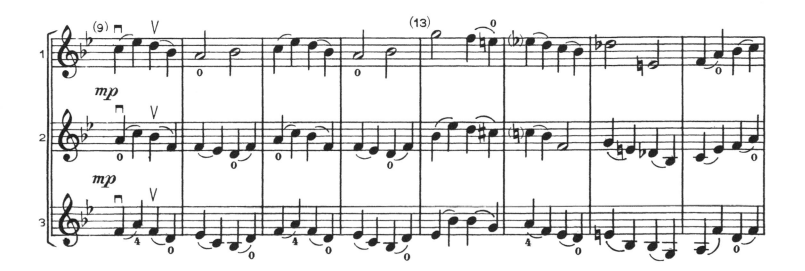

Trio Elégante

Legato

* *Con sordini 1st time*
** *Senza sordini 2nd time*

BLUMENTHAL

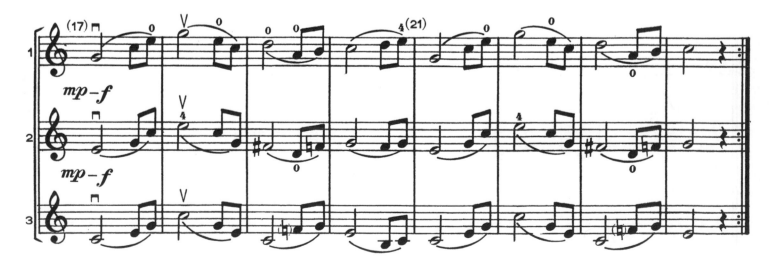

* *Con sordini*: With the mutes.   ** *Senza sordini*: Without the mutes.

Trio-Novellette

EICHBERG

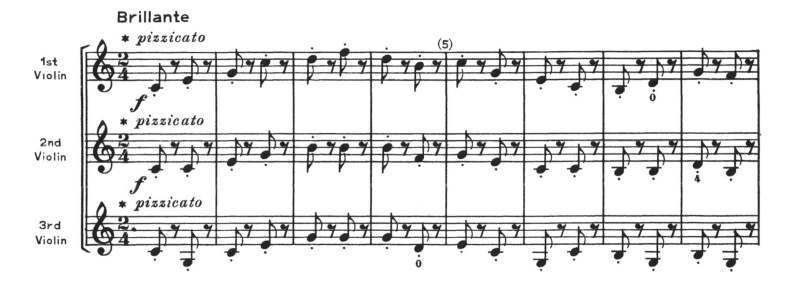

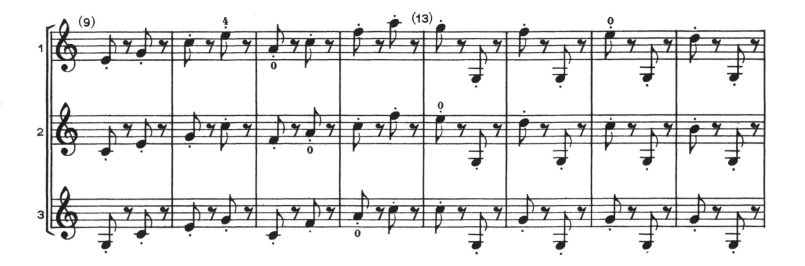

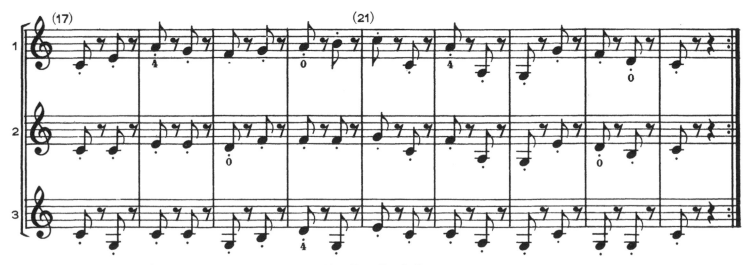

* *pizzicato* or *pizz.* = Pluck the string with the first finger.

Trio Dramatique

BLUMENTHAL

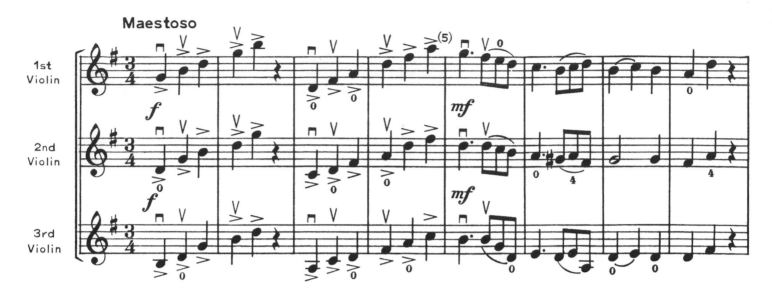

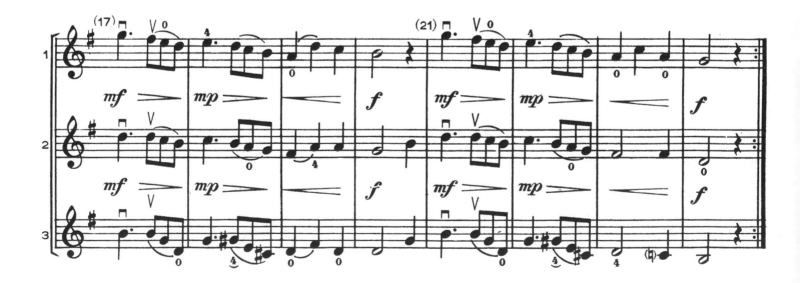

1363-31

Trio de Ballet

HOFFMANN

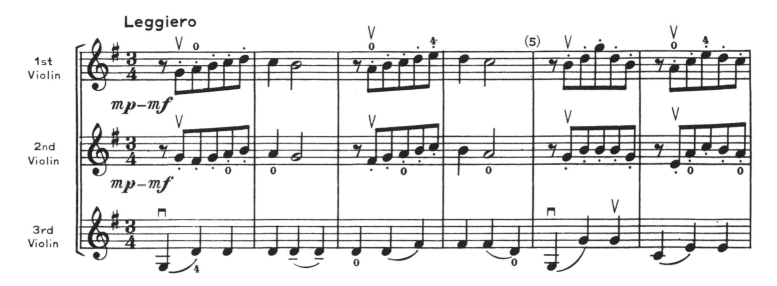

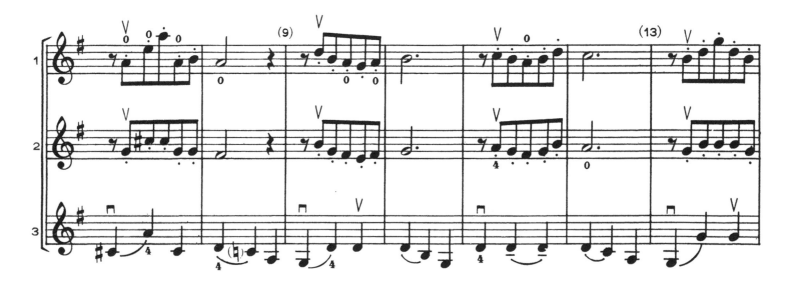

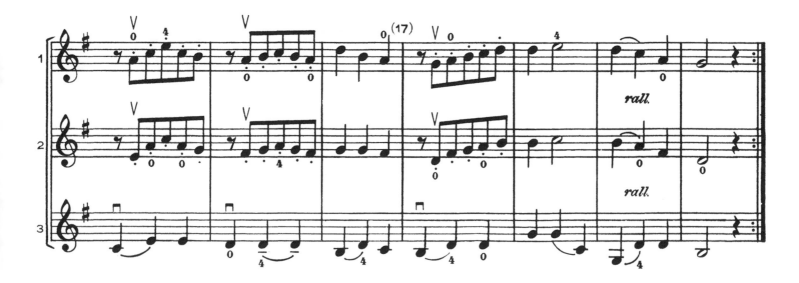

Trio Populaire

EICHBERG

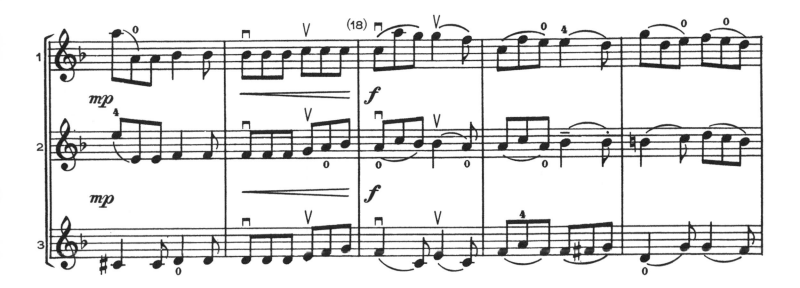

Trio Brillante

DANCLA

Scintillante

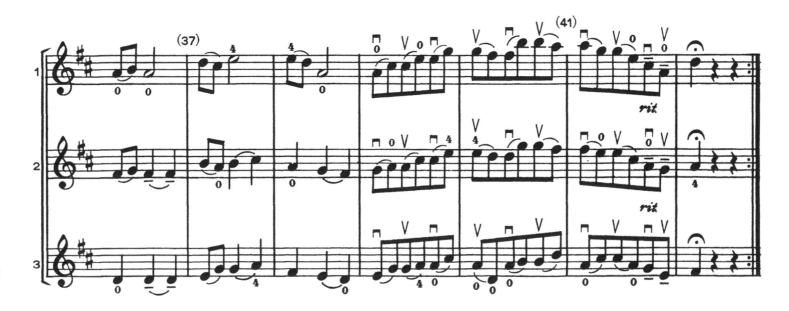

Trio Divertimento

EICHBERG

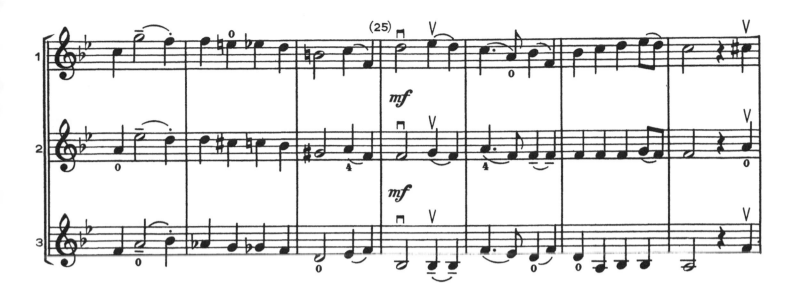

Trio Perpetuo

TOURS

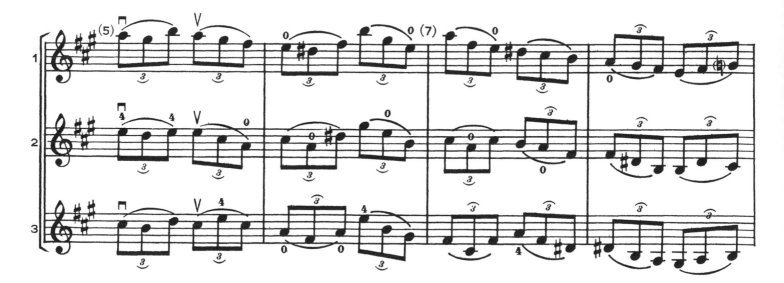

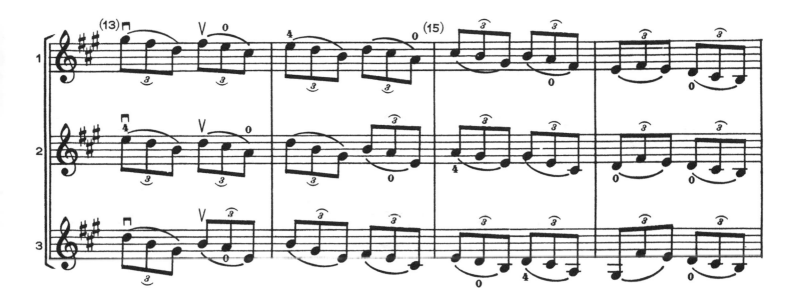

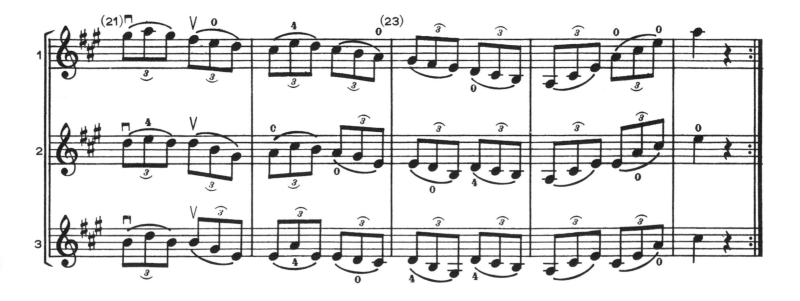

Trio-Impromptu

HOFFMANN

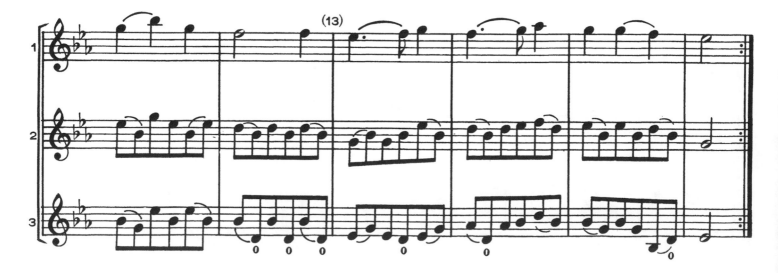

Trio Lyrique

DE BERIOT

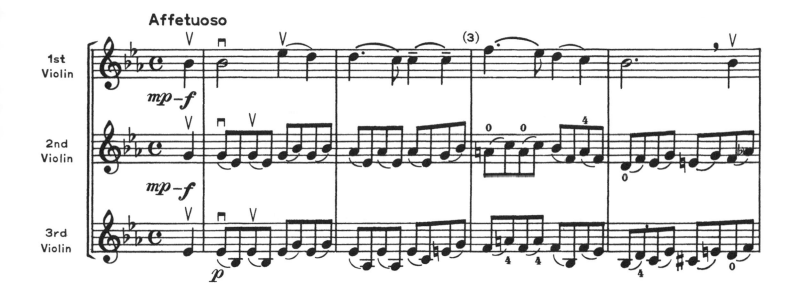

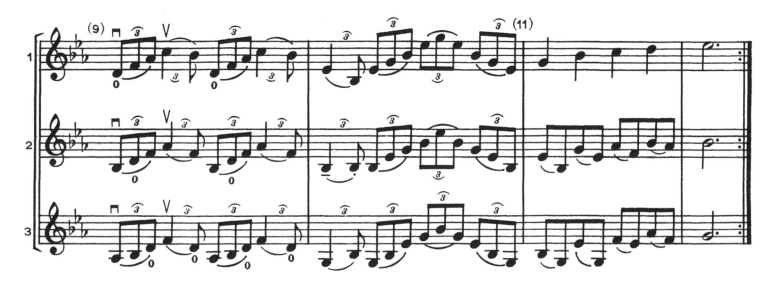

1363-31

Trio Scherzando

HERMANN

Con anima

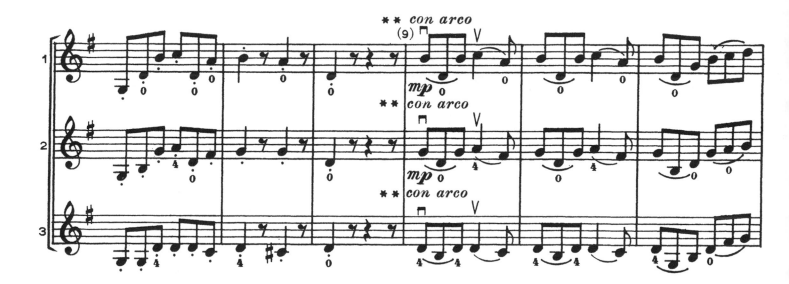

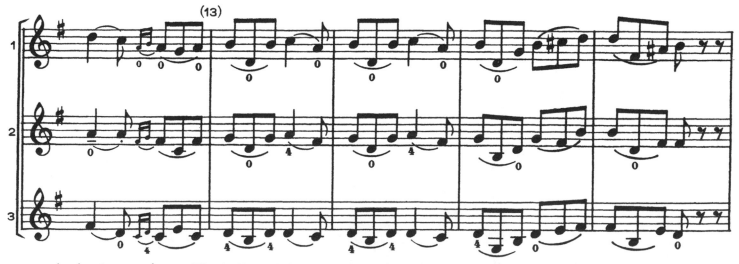

* *pizzicato*, or *pizz.* = Pluck the string with the first finger.

** *con arco*, or *arco.* = Play with the bow.

Trio - Finale

TOURS

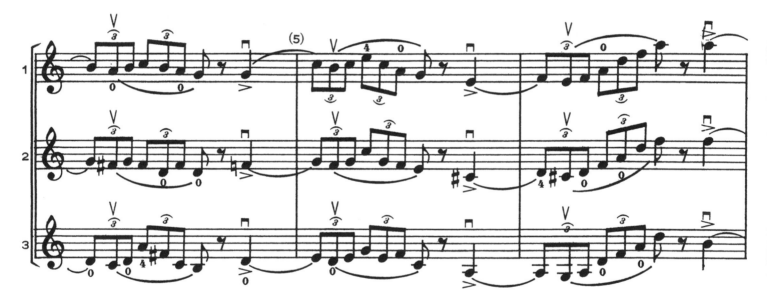